Breaking The Debt Ceiling

David Ehlers

Published by KalPrint Books
Kalgoorlie, Western Australia
First Edition – 2025

Cover design, interior layout, and formatting by KalPrint Books

Table of Contents

Foreword

Freedom Is God's Desire

Debt is one of the most quietly destructive forces in modern life. It rarely arrives suddenly or dramatically. More often, it creeps in gradually—through small decisions, delayed repayments, unexpected hardships, or seasons of survival that stretch longer than we ever intended. Before long, what once felt manageable becomes heavy, and what once seemed temporary begins to feel permanent.

For many people, debt is not merely a financial issue. It affects peace of mind, family relationships, decision-making, generosity, and even spiritual confidence. It has the power to shape our future and restrict our freedom. That is why Scripture speaks so clearly about it—not to condemn, but to restore.

This book is not about get-rich-quick formulas or financial shortcuts. It is a study rooted in Scripture, built around one powerful and practical passage: **2 Kings 4:1–7**. In this account, we meet a widow who is faithful, fearful, overwhelmed, and trapped by debt. Her situation is desperate. Her options are limited. Yet her story becomes a timeless picture of how God brings freedom—not through magic, but through obedience, order, and faith in action.

What is striking about this passage is that God's miracle did not remove responsibility. Instead, it required participation. The widow had to take inventory, follow instruction, involve her household, and act consistently until the work was complete. God provided the oil, but she had to pour it. God made a way, but she had to walk it.

That same pattern runs throughout Scripture. God is not opposed to provision, but He is deeply committed to stewardship. He does not free His people so they can return to bondage, but so they can live with peace, purpose, and integrity. Financial freedom, in the biblical sense, is not about abundance for indulgence—it is about liberty for obedience.

As you read this book, you will be challenged to look honestly at your finances, your habits, and your priorities. At times, that honesty may be uncomfortable. But discomfort is often the doorway to change. This is not a call to shame, but a call to responsibility. Not a message of guilt, but of hope. God's desire has always been freedom for His people, freedom from fear, from bondage, and from anything that competes with trust in Him.

Whether you are deeply in debt, carrying a manageable load, or simply wanting to live wisely and intentionally, this book invites you into a process. Not a perfect process, but a faithful one. Step by step, chapter by chapter, it will walk you through recognition, inventory, movement, structure, perseverance, and obedience.

Freedom rarely comes all at once. But it always comes to those who are willing to obey God's instruction and stay the course.

My prayer is that this study will not only help you break the debt ceiling in your life, but also strengthen your trust in God, deepen your discipline, and restore peace to your household. Freedom is not a fantasy. It is God's desire, and with His help, it is possible.

Introduction

Every nation, household, and individual face a limit, a ceiling, that restricts how far they can go when debt is left unchecked. In the financial world, a "debt ceiling" is a cap set to prevent spending beyond what is sustainable. Yet in everyday life, many people quietly break through their own ceilings, spending more than they earn, borrowing beyond their capacity, and living in the bondage of debt.

This book, "Breaking the Debt Ceiling", is a study drawn from 2 Kings 4:1–7, where a desperate widow faces the crushing weight of inherited debt. Her story not only reveals the pain of financial pressure but also the redemptive power of faith, obedience, and divine provision. Through her experience, we uncover biblical principles that challenge us to live within our means, reject the lies of materialism, and embrace God's strategy for breakthrough.

Whether you're burdened by financial strain or seeking wisdom to live responsibly, this book will inspire you to take practical steps of faith toward freedom. It's time to stop spending beyond the boundary, and start trusting God to "break the ceiling" and supply every need.

The Story

'A certain woman of the wives of the sons of the prophets cried out to Elisha, saying, "Your servant my husband is dead, and you know that your servant feared the Lord. And the creditor is coming to take my two sons to be his slaves." So Elisha said to her, "What shall I do for you? Tell me, what do you have in the house?" And she said, "Your maidservant has nothing in the house but a jar of oil." Then he said, "Go, borrow vessels from everywhere, from all your neighbours, empty vessels; do not gather just a few. And when you have come in, you shall shut the door behind you and your sons; then pour it into all those vessels, and set aside the full ones." So she went from him and shut the door behind her and her sons, who brought the vessels to her; and she poured it out. Now it came to pass, when the vessels were full, that she said to her son, "Bring me another vessel." And he said to her, "There is not another vessel." So the oil ceased. Then she came and told the man of God. And he said, "Go, sell the oil and pay your debt; and you and your sons live on the rest."'

2 Kings 4:1-7

1

Chapter 1: Debt Reality

'A certain woman of the wives of the sons of the prophets cried out to Elisha, saying, "Your servant my husband is dead, and you know that your servant feared the Lord. And the creditor is coming to take my two sons to be his slaves."'

2 Kings 4:1

We live in a world overwhelmed by debt. From personal loans and credit cards to national deficits and economic bailouts, debt has become a normal part of life. Many people today find themselves trapped in financial burdens that seem impossible to escape. But the Bible is not silent on this issue. It offers a clear and powerful answer, God's plan for becoming free from the grip of debt.

Debt is never presented as neutral in Scripture.
In the Bible, debt is consistently linked to loss of freedom, diminished authority, and compromised inheritance. While God shows compassion toward those trapped in debt, He never celebrates it as normal or healthy. From Genesis to Revelation, freedom is God's design, and bondage, financial or otherwise, is something He seeks to break.

"The alien who is among you shall rise higher and higher above you, and you shall come down lower and lower. He shall lend to you, but you shall not lend to him; he shall be the head, and you shall be the tail."
(Deuteronomy 28:43-44)

In this study titled "Breaking the Debt Ceiling", we explore the idea that, just like governments impose a spending limit to avoid exceeding a debt threshold, we too must learn to live within our means and follow God's guidance in financial matters. We begin with the story found in 2 Kings 4:1–7, where a desperate widow finds herself in a debt crisis. Her story reveals the reality of debt, its power, and God's redemptive plan.

The Reality of Life

Life has a way of taking unexpected turns. Even the most faithful believers can find themselves behind financially, facing debts that feel insurmountable. The widow in 2 Kings 4:1 cried out to the prophet Elisha. "Your servant my husband is dead, and you know that your servant feared the Lord. And the creditor is coming to take my two sons to be his slaves." (2 Kings 4:1, NKJV)

She had already experienced the devastating loss of her husband. Now, with creditors knocking at her door, she was about to lose her sons as well. Her sons represented her hope, her future, and that was on the verge of being taken away.

This is not a unique story. In 1 Samuel 22:2, we read that when David was fleeing from King Saul, he was joined by many men. "And everyone who was in distress, everyone who was in debt, and everyone who was discontented gathered to him. So he became captain over them." (1 Samuel 22:2, NKJV)

These were broken men, many burdened by debt. And yet, from this troubled group, many would go on to become David's mighty men.

In Nehemiah 5:1–5, God's people cried out because debt had forced them to mortgage their land and sell their children into servitude. Though they were rebuilding Jerusalem, they were being destroyed economically from within. This shows us that debt doesn't just affect individuals, it erodes families, communities, and spiritual momentum.

"Just because you're in a storm doesn't mean you're not in God's will."

—Tony Evans

The message is clear: being in debt doesn't mean your story is over. You still have a future. As Jeremiah 29:11 declares. "For I know the thoughts that I think toward you, says the Lord, thoughts of peace and not of evil, to give you a future and a hope." (Jeremiah 29:11, NKJV)

We see this reflected in the life of Stacey Little. On the very day his son was born, Stacey declared bankruptcy. Raised in poverty and overwhelmed by financial setbacks, he felt trapped, until he began blogging about Southern cooking. What started as a passion project eventually became "Southern Bite", a successful online business that now generates seven-figure revenue. His story reminds us that a future is possible, even when the present seems bleak.

God knew that debt would be a reality for many of His people, so He included guidance in His Word. In Deuteronomy 15:1–5, God commanded that debts be forgiven every seven years. This wasn't just a financial reset; it was a spiritual principle of grace and redemption. God promised blessing for those who obeyed His instruction. "You will receive this blessing if you are careful to obey all the commands of the Lord your God that I am giving you today." (Deuteronomy 15:5, NLT)

Even faithful, God-fearing people are not exempt from the trials of life. The widow's husband had feared the Lord, yet debt still found its way into their home. As 1 Peter 4:12 reminds us. "Beloved, do not think it strange concerning the fiery trial which is to try you, as though some strange thing happened to you." (1 Peter 4:12, NKJV)

The Power of Debt

Debt has a devastating power. It doesn't merely impact our wallets; it reaches into every area of life. The Message paraphrase of 2 Kings 4:1 puts it starkly. "One day the wife of a man from the guild of prophets called out to Elisha, 'Your servant my husband is dead… the man to whom he was in debt is on his way to collect by taking my two children as slaves.'"

Debt had already stolen her husband through hardship, and now it threatened to take her children. It takes without remorse. In Matthew 18:28–30, Jesus told a parable about a man who demanded repayment from a fellow servant. "He laid hands on him and took him by the throat, saying, 'Pay me what you owe!' … and threw him into prison till he should pay the debt." (Matthew 18:28–30, NKJV)

"Why Debt Matters to God"

1. **Debt threatens inheritance**
    - **Proverbs 13:22** "A good man leaves an inheritance to his children's children"
    - The widow's sons represented future provision
2. **Debt restricts obedience**
    - **Luke 16:10–11** "He who is faithful in what is least is faithful also in much; and he who is unjust in what is least is unjust also in much. Therefore if you have not been faithful in the unrighteous mammon, who will commit to your trust the true riches?"
    - When finances rule us, God doesn't fully
3. **Debt creates dependence on man instead of God**
    - **Psalm 118:8** "It is better to trust in the Lord Than to put confidence in man."

We see the impact of debt in the present. Proverbs 6:3–4 urges. "Go and humble yourself; plead with your friend. Give no sleep to your eyes, nor slumber to your eyelids." (Proverbs 6:3–4, NKJV)

The stress of owing money often robs us of rest and joy.

Proverbs 22:27 (NLT) paints a vivid picture. "If you can't pay it, even your bed will be snatched from under you."

Debt doesn't stop at the present; it devours the future. The widow's sons, her only means of support and legacy, were on the verge of being taken. She cried. "A man he owed money to has come to take away my two sons as slaves in payment for my husband's debt." (2 Kings 4:1, GNT)

Chris, a man who once owed $47,000 in credit card debt, shares this reality. His income barely covered the interest, and he lived with constant anxiety, unable to focus on long-term goals. Through credit counselling, disciplined budgeting, and faith, he slowly paid off the debt. Today, he testifies of restored peace and renewed vision for his future.

Jesus taught that the one forgiven much loves much. This reveals that debt is not just about obligation, it affects our heart posture. When people remain trapped in debt, it can distort gratitude, generosity, and spiritual freedom.

"Debt is the slavery of the free."

—Publilius Syrus

Debt rarely begins as rebellion, it usually begins as permission. A small compromise, a delayed payment, a justified purchase. But over time, what we allow quietly becomes what controls us. Scripture repeatedly warns that what we tolerate today will dominate us tomorrow.

"Catch us the foxes, The little foxes that spoil the vines, For our vines have tender grapes."
(Song of Solomon 2:15)

"When you get in debt, you become a servant. The borrower is servant to the lender. That's biblical, and that's real."

—Dave Ramsey

God's Plan

Praise God, He has a plan for our freedom. He does not want His people trapped in financial bondage. In Matthew 18:27 (NCV), Jesus described a master who forgave a servant's enormous debt "The master felt sorry for his servant and told him he did not have to pay it back. Then he let the servant go free."

God wants to release us, restore us, and provide for us. Philippians 4:19 assures us. "And my God shall supply all your need according to His riches in glory by Christ Jesus." (Philippians 4:19, NKJV)

But God's provision often requires our participation. To get out of debt, we must trust His plan and act on His instruction. Isaiah 41:10 encourages us. "Fear not, for I am with you… I will strengthen you, Yes, I will help you." (Isaiah 41:10, NKJV)

And again, in verse 13. "For I, the Lord your God, will hold your right hand, saying to you, 'Fear not, I will help you.'" (Isaiah 41:13, NKJV)

Brittany and Andrew experienced this firsthand. Struggling under $10,000 of credit card debt, they felt God leading them to empty their small savings account and pay it off in full. Though scared, they obeyed. Within weeks, unexpected income and blessings began pouring in. Their step of faith opened the door to financial freedom.

"Financial freedom is available to those who learn about it and work for it."

—Robert Kiyosaki

"God's plan is not just to rescue us from debt, but to lead us into abundance with wisdom."

–Unknown

This study is a roadmap. It's not about formulas, but about faith. If we walk in obedience and trust God's guidance, He will lead us out of debt. Romans 13:8 calls us to a new way of living. "Owe no one anything except to love one another, for he who loves another has fulfilled the law." (Romans 13:8, NKJV)

Let this chapter be your starting point. No matter where you are, God can bring you through. You can break the debt ceiling, not by willpower alone, but through God's plan, His promises, and His power.

For group discussion questions and personal reflection related to this chapter, please see the Small Group & Personal Study Guide in the Appendix.

Chapter 2: What's in Your House?

"So Elisha said to her, 'What shall I do for you? Tell me, what do you have in the house?' And she said, 'Your maidservant has nothing in the house but a jar of oil.'"

2 Kings 4:2

Debt is a familiar burden in our world, personal debt, national debt, even generational debt. For many, it feels like a trap with no way out. But the Bible provides clear direction for financial freedom, and the story of the widow in 2 Kings 4:1–7 offers more than just inspiration, it gives us practical insight into God's method for breaking the chains of debt.

In this chapter, we're faced with a fundamental question. What's in your house? The key to reversing financial strain often begins not with what we don't have, but with what we already do.

Throughout Scripture, God rarely begins with what people lack. Instead, He consistently begins with what they already possess. This pattern reveals a foundational principle of faith. God is not limited by the size of our resources, but by our willingness to surrender them. Before God multiplies, He identifies. Before He adds, He asks.

Looking in the Wrong Place

When the widow's crisis reached its peak, she turned to the prophet Elisha for help. His response was striking: "How can I help you? Tell me, what do you have in your house?" (2 Kings 4:2 NCV). Her answer was modest, "I have nothing except a pot of oil." *It*'s a familiar scenario. Like this widow, we often look outside ourselves for rescue, hoping someone else will fix our debt or ease our burden. But Elisha directed her attention inward, not outward.

When God called Moses, He didn't give him something new. He asked, "What is that in your hand?" (Exodus 4:2). Moses answered, "A rod." It was ordinary, familiar, unimpressive. Yet once surrendered, that rod became the instrument of miracles, authority, and deliverance. God didn't replace what Moses had. He repurposed it.

In John 6:9 we read the disciples response to Jesus asking them, *"what do you have in your hand"*. "There is a lad here who has five barley loaves and two small fish..." They said we have nothing, but they did have something, that something is what God multiplied.

"When we depend on man, we get what man can do. When we depend on prayer, we get what God can do."

—A.C. Dixon

Many today are guilty of the same misdirection. We look for easy solutions, hoping for a financial bailout, a loan, or someone else to shoulder the burden. But God's method begins with personal responsibility and a willingness to seek His help.

I remember a conversation with My Pastor many years ago. I approached him for some financial help, and his reply was simple yet convicting. "Dave, you're asking the wrong person. You need to ask God." That wisdom has stayed with me. Whether it's about debt or financial breakthrough, our first step must be toward God, not man.

"God never leads us to where His grace cannot keep us or His power cannot provide for us."

—Unknown

"And you shall remember the Lord your God, for it is He who gives you power to get wealth, that He may establish His covenant..." Deuteronomy 8:18

Sometimes, we're not really looking for God's help, we're hoping for a quick fix that costs us nothing. The widow's initial instinct was for Elisha to simply "fix" her problem, but Elisha wasn't there to provide a handout. He was there to connect her to a "miracle", and that required her involvement.

"Too many people miss the silver lining because they're expecting gold."

—Maurice Setter

Many avoid doing the hard work, prayer, fasting, sacrifice, making practical changes, because it's uncomfortable. But James 4:2 makes it clear, "...You do not have because you do not ask." We often look in the wrong place when the right help has always been God's way.

Looking at the Wrong Things

When Elisha asked the widow what she had, her immediate response was, *"I have nothing."* This is a common reaction in financial distress. Debt can cloud our view of reality until all we see is lack. We convince ourselves that we have nothing of value, that the situation is too big and that even God can't help.

"Faith is not the belief that God will do what you want. It is the belief that God will do what is right."

—Max Lucado

"Look, if the Lord would make windows in heaven, could this thing be?" (2 Kings 7:2)

These words, spoken in disbelief during a time of famine, capture how many people feel about their finances. When we fix our eyes on the wrong things, three major consequences follow:

We lose faith.

We forget that God is for us, that He is willing and able to help.

"The Lord is my helper; I will not fear. What can man do to me?" (Hebrews 13:6)

"And my God shall supply all your need according to His riches in glory by Christ Jesus." (Philippians 4:19)

"When you change the way you look at things, the things you look at change."

—Wayne Dyer

We lose hope.

When the widow said, "I have nothing," it reflected a resignation of hope. That mindset is dangerous.

"Hope deferred makes the heart sick, but when the desire comes, it is a tree of life." (Proverbs 13:12)

Many people give up too soon. They've tried before, failed, and now refuse to try again.

"That is hopeless! So we will walk according to our own plans..."(Jeremiah 18:12)

"Hope is being able to see that there is light despite all the darkness."

—Desmond Tutu

We lose perspective.

The widow couldn't see the value in what she had. But God specializes in using small things to create miracles.

"Ah, Lord God! Behold, You have made the heavens and the earth... There is nothing too hard for You." (Jeremiah 32:17)
"Is anything too hard for the Lord?" (Genesis 18:14)
"The bin of flour was not used up, nor did the jar of oil run dry..." (1 Kings 17:16)

"The real voyage of discovery consists not in seeking new landscapes, but in having new eyes."

—Marcel Proust

Looking at What's in Your House

Elisha's question was more than practical, it was prophetic. "What do you have in your house?" It was a question that forced the widow to take inventory. And it's the same question God asks us today.

What do you already have that God can use to begin reversing your financial condition? Do you have skills you're not using? Resources you've overlooked. Items you could sell to eliminate debt.

"Start where you are. Use what you have. Do what you can."

—Arthur Ashe

Sometimes, the answer is as simple as this: if you own three cars and only need two, sell one. If you have credit cards digging you deeper into debt, cut them up. Freedom starts with what you have.

This principle isn't just biblical, it's proven in real life.

A few years ago, a single mother in the United States found herself in a financial crisis. Her job didn't pay enough to cover her bills, and credit card debt was piling up. She considered taking out a loan or asking family members for help, but she didn't want to go deeper into debt. One night, while praying in desperation, she felt God prompt her with a question. "What do you have in your house?" At first, her mind went blank. She thought, "I have nothing." But then she remembered, she had a small oven, a few baking supplies, and a talent for making cakes. It wasn't much. But she decided to bake a few cupcakes and post photos on Facebook. To her surprise, people started placing orders. Word spread in her community. Soon, she was selling cakes for birthdays, weddings, and baby showers. Within a year, she was earning enough to pay off her credit cards. Today, her home-based bakery has grown into a small business with two part-time employees, and she runs it while still being home with her kids. What changed? She stopped looking at what she lacked, and started seeing what she already had. Like the widow in 2 Kings 4, her miracle began the moment she took inventory and allowed God to multiply what was in her house.

"God will always use what you have to create what you need."

Steven Furtick

"But let each one examine his own work…" (Galatians 6:4)

Before God multiplies, He requires clarity.

- What income actually comes in?
- Where does it really go?
- What expenses are necessary, and which are tolerated?

"Be diligent to know the state of your flocks, and attend to your herds." (Proverbs 27:23)

In Bible times, flocks represented wealth and stability. Today, that means your financial portfolio, your assets, your income and expenses. Do you know the state of your finances? Have you sat down and examined:

- What do I have?
- What do I owe?

- What can I contribute to reducing my debt?

These are uncomfortable questions, but they are necessary ones. Breaking the debt ceiling is not about waiting for a miracle, it's about participating in one. God will bless what you surrender, but He starts with what's already in your house.

"The miracle is not in what you don't have; the miracle is in what you already possess."

—Unknown

God will not multiply what we refuse to manage. If we continually ignore, misuse, or waste what He has already entrusted to us, we limit what He can do next. Stewardship is not about perfection, it's about honesty.

"Success comes not from having more, but from doing more with what you already have."

—John C. Maxwell

So what do you have?

For group discussion questions and personal reflection related to this chapter, please see the Small Group & Personal Study Guide in the Appendix.

Chapter 3: Moving Toward Freedom

Then he said, "Go, borrow vessels from everywhere, from all your neighbours, empty vessels; do not gather just a few."

2 Kings 4:3

Up to this point, we've identified the problem of debt and the resources God has already placed in our hands. But recognition alone does not bring freedom. At some point, faith must move from awareness to action. In this chapter, we see that freedom begins when we move, intentionally, decisively, and obediently, toward what God has promised.

Debt is a reality that touches nearly every part of our society, personal debt, national debt, and everything in between. Many individuals find themselves weighed down by financial burdens that seem impossible to break. Yet the Bible offers more than hope, it offers a plan. In our study of Breaking the Debt Ceiling, we've been exploring how God's Word provides the keys to financial freedom. In this chapter, we focus on how to move toward freedom, by setting the right priorities, cultivating the right relationships, and maintaining the right attitude.

The Right Priority

The widow in 2 Kings 4 had one goal, to eliminate her debt. Elisha's instruction to sell the oil and "pay your debt; and you and your sons live on the rest" (verse 7) makes it clear, debt repayment had to come first. This was not a suggestion; it was a command of priority.

She was not to use the proceeds to take a vacation, buy new clothes, or treat herself. Every drop of oil, every cent gained, was directed at one thing, freedom from debt. Until that was accomplished, nothing else mattered.

"When you get your priorities straight, everything else falls into place."

—Zig Ziglar

Solomon echoes this urgency in Proverbs 6:1–4, warning that if you've become ensnared by financial obligations, "give no sleep to your eyes, nor slumber to your eyelids", until you're free. Debt is not a casual matter in Scripture. It's something to be escaped from, urgently.

One inspiring real-life example of this kind of priority shift is Alex Wren, a single mother from South Yorkshire. By age 22, she was £15,000 in credit card debt despite working minimum wage jobs and spending freely. Everything changed when she became pregnant and realized that continuing her financial habits would leave her trapped. She set her sights on one goal: paying off her debt. By committing to a strict budget and monetizing her social media, she was completely debt-free within two years. Today, she earns over £50,000 annually and teaches others the importance of making debt elimination a top priority.

"The man who never has money enough to pay his debts has too much of something else."

—James Lendall Basford

Even the Law of Moses emphasized debt release every seven years (Deuteronomy 15:1–2), showing that freedom from financial bondage is part of God's heart for His people.

God's plan is for us to be the lender, not the borrower, the head, not the tail (Deuteronomy 28:13). Yet as long as we remain in debt, we remain servants to the lender (Proverbs 22:7).

"You must gain control over your money or the lack of it will forever control you."

—Dave Ramsey

Our ability to give generously, the very thing that activates God's increase in our lives, is hindered until we're free. 2 Corinthians 9:6 reminds us, "He who sows sparingly will also reap sparingly, and he who sows bountifully will also reap bountifully."

"A budget is telling your money where to go instead of wondering where it went."

—Dave Ramsey

The Right Connections

The widow could not have achieved freedom on her own. Elisha told her to go and borrow empty vessels, not just a few, from her neighbours (2 Kings 4:3, NCV). Her miracle required the involvement of others.

"You can't do it alone, and you're not meant to."

—John C. Maxwell

This highlights the power of relationships. In moments of financial distress, the strength of our connections often determines the reach of our recovery. Her neighbours had to be willing to help, but that willingness likely came from how she had treated them in the past. Proverbs 18:24 reminds us, "A man who has friends must himself be friendly."

"Surround yourself with people who lift you higher."

—Oprah Winfrey

One modern story that beautifully illustrates this is Ayesha O'Neill, the owner of Rito's Cafe in South Australia. Facing closure due to a $20,000 debt and having not drawn a wage in almost a year, she made a heartfelt appeal to her community. Her long-standing relationships, generosity, and care for her staff paid off, locals rallied around her, supporting her through a GoFundMe campaign. Her story reveals how crucial good connections can be in turning crisis into comeback.

"The richest people in the world build networks; everyone else is trained to look for work."

—Robert Kiyosaki

"A friend is one who walks in when others walk out."

—Walter Winchell

The widow's story would have ended in despair without the borrowed jars. Just as her connections enabled the miracle, our relationships matter more than we often realize.

"Two are better than one... if either of them falls, the one will lift up his companion." Ecclesiastes 4:9–10

Just as the right connections can accelerate freedom, the wrong ones can quietly sabotage it. Some voices normalize debt, mock discipline, or pressure us into spending we can't afford. Moving toward freedom sometimes means limiting access, not just increasing support.

"He who walks with wise men will be wise, But the companion of fools will be destroyed."
(Proverbs 13:20)

The Right Attitude

Finally, if we are to move toward financial freedom, our attitude must reflect seriousness and full commitment. Elisha told the widow, "Don't ask for just a few [jars]" (2 Kings 4:3, NCV). This wasn't a time for hesitation or half-hearted effort, it was a time to go all in.

"You will never change your life until you change something you do daily."

—John C. Maxwell

Scripture never presents breakthrough as instant; it presents it as faithful. The widow didn't pour once, she poured until there were no more vessels. Freedom came not from a moment of enthusiasm, but from sustained obedience.

"For you have need of endurance, so that after you have done the will of God, you may receive the promise:" (Hebrews 10:36)

That's the mindset we need. Not "I'll try to pay off a little," or "Maybe I'll clear it someday." But rather, "I'm not stopping until this is gone." There must be determination, a refusal to tolerate lingering debt.

"Your attitude, not your aptitude, will determine your altitude."

—Zig Ziglar

Consider the story of Bernadette Joy, a first-generation American who found herself buried under $300,000 in debt. Though she followed all the conventional wisdom, get a degree, work hard, invest, she still felt like a slave to debt. What changed her life wasn't just financial advice; it was her attitude. She sold unnecessary possessions, lived below her means, picked upside hustles, and tackled the debt aggressively. Her mindset shift made all the difference. Today, she teaches others how to find financial freedom through relentless commitment.

"Success is not for the lazy. If you want to win, you've got to commit."

—Eric Thomas

Jesus spoke in Matthew 18:34 of a servant who was delivered to torturers until he repaid all he owed. Though spiritual in context, the principle is this, avoiding our obligations has serious consequences.

"Act as if what you do makes a difference. It does."

—William James

"Let us not grow weary while doing good, for in due season we shall reap if we do not lose heart."

Galatians 6:9

The pathway to financial freedom isn't paved with luck, wishful thinking, or short-term gimmicks. It's built on God's principles, making debt repayment a priority, leaning into the relationships He's placed around us, and having an attitude that refuses to quit.

Just as the widow's oil didn't stop flowing until the last borrowed jar was filled, God's provision continues when we faithfully act on His Word. The ceiling can break, but we must first break away from the mindsets and habits that keep us beneath it.

Moving toward freedom does not mean the journey will be quick or painless. The widow still had to borrow vessels, shut the door, and pour until exhaustion. But movement changes everything. When you move toward obedience, heaven joins the process.

"And it shall come to pass, as soon as the soles of the feet of the priests who bear the ark of the Lord, the Lord of all the earth, shall rest in the waters of the Jordan, that the waters of

the Jordan shall be cut off, the waters that come down from upstream, and they shall stand as a heap." So it was, when the people set out from their camp to cross over the Jordan, with the priests bearing the ark of the covenant before the people, and as those who bore the ark came to the Jordan, and the feet of the priests who bore the ark dipped in the edge of the water (for the Jordan overflows all its banks during the whole time of harvest), that the waters which came down from upstream stood still, and rose in a heap very far away at Adam, the city that is beside Zaretan. So the waters that went down into the Sea of the Arabah, the Salt Sea, failed, and were cut off; and the people crossed over opposite Jericho. Then the priests who bore the ark of the covenant of the Lord stood firm on dry ground in the midst of the Jordan; and all Israel crossed over on dry ground, until all the people had crossed completely over the Jordan."
(Joshua 3:13-17)

God did not remove the obstacle before they moved. He removed it because they moved. In the same way, financial freedom often follows obedience, not precedes it.

You're not meant to live under the weight of debt forever. With God's help, you can move toward freedom.

"Therefore if the Son makes you free, you shall be free indeed."
(John 8:36)

For group discussion questions and personal reflection related to this chapter, please see the Small Group & Personal Study Guide in the Appendix.

Chapter 4: Planning, Preventing, & Producing

And when you have come in, you shall shut the door behind you and your sons; then pour it into all those vessels, and set aside the full ones.

2 Kings 4:4

Debt is a reality many people face, whether it's personal, national, or somewhere in between. But God gives us a clear roadmap for getting free. In our study of Breaking the Debt Ceiling, we've seen that just like a national debt ceiling limits spending, we must learn to live within our means and apply biblical wisdom to our finances.

God is not a God of confusion, chaos, or randomness. Throughout Scripture, He works through order, structure, and obedience. Miracles may be supernatural, but they are rarely unstructured. Before God multiplies, He organizes. Before He provides, He prepares.

1 Corinthians 14:40 – "Let all things be done decently and in order"

In this chapter, we look at three powerful principles from the story in 2 Kings 4.
Planning, Preventing, and Producing. These are the keys that unlock the door to financial freedom.

The Power of Planning

Planning is one of the Bible's most practical financial principles. When we face debt, we need a plan, and that plan is often called a budget. As John C. Maxwell puts it, *"A budget is telling your money where to go instead of wondering where it went."*

Proverbs 21:5 says it well, "Good planning and hard work lead to prosperity, but hasty shortcuts lead to poverty." (NCV)

There's a well-known story from Dave Ramsey's teachings about a couple who paid off over $100,000 in debt. They started small, writing down every expense, eating rice and beans, cutting up credit cards, and taking second jobs. With consistent planning and sacrifice, they became debt-free in under three years.

In our Scripture, Elisha tells the widow to collect vessels and prepare to pour. He essentially says, Get everything ready, have a plan, then we'll start the miracle.

Faith does not replace planning; it directs it. Presumption assumes God will cover what we refuse to prepare for. Planning is not a lack of faith, it is faith applied wisely. In Luke 14:28–30 Jesus spoke about "Counting the cost". And Proverbs 27:12 The Bible says that "the prudent foresee danger".

Planning brings focus. It gives us something to aim at. As Paul wrote in Philippians 3:13–14, "I press toward the goal for the prize of the upward call of God in Christ Jesus." A goal keeps our eyes on the prize: freedom from debt.

Joseph didn't wait for famine to strike before planning. He stored during abundance so that lack wouldn't destroy the future. This mirrors Elisha's instruction: prepare the vessels first, then pour.

Planning also brings clarity. We start to see what needs to change, maybe it's cutting up the credit cards, taking on extra work, or learning to live on less. Psalm 119:73 reminds us, "Give me understanding, that I may learn Your commandments."

Take Angela, a single mum from Ohio, who was drowning in $30,000 of debt and facing foreclosure. She took a financial course at church, created a "debt snowball," used cash jars, and committed to no new spending. She paid it all off in four years, all because she had a clear plan.

The Power of Prevention

Once we have a plan, we need to close the door on anything that could derail it. Elisha told the widow, "Shut the door behind you and your sons." That wasn't just a privacy measure, it was a powerful image of shutting out distractions, temptations, and anything that would lead her back into debt.

Prevention in Scripture is proactive, not reactive. God often tells His people what to avoid before He tells them what to pursue. Closing the door is not weakness, it's wisdom.

The Bible addresses boundary setting, Proverbs 4:23, admonishes "Guard your heart
Job 31:1 Job declared a boundary in his life, "I made a covenant with my eyes"

For us, that might mean saying no to new credit cards, cutting off unnecessary subscriptions, or staying away from shops and online sales.

As Dave Ramsey says, "If you want to be wealthy, you have to stop doing what broke people do."

James and Kelly from Georgia did exactly that. With over $80,000 in debt, they had a "debt funeral," cutting up all their cards, unsubscribing from shopping emails, and using only cash. That one decision to "shut the door" became the turning point in their journey.

Romans 13:14 says, "Put on the Lord Jesus Christ, and make no provision for the flesh." That's exactly what this means, no provision for more debt.

But shutting the door also means unity. Elisha said, "Shut the door behind you and your sons." Everyone in the household needed to be on the same page. If one person is budgeting while another is spending freely, the plan won't work.

Amos 3:3 asks, "Can two walk together unless they are agreed?"

In 2019, a family of five in Sydney shared their journey on a financial TV show. They involved everyone, children included, in budgeting and saving. One child tracked grocery spending, another monitored power use. Together, they paid off $40,000 in just 18 months. The father said, "When the door shut behind us, we were all inside, working the plan together."

The Power of Production

Once the plan is in place and the door is shut, it's time to do the work. Elisha tells the woman, "Then pour it into all those vessels, and set aside the full ones." In other words, start pouring.

Good intentions won't pay off your debt. You have to act. Zig Ziglar said, "You don't have to be great to start, but you have to start to be great."

"He who has a slack hand becomes poor, But the hand of the diligent makes rich."
(Proverbs 10:4)

God does not bless passivity. He blesses faithful effort. Pouring required repetition, energy, and endurance. Miracles often happen while hands are moving.

James 2:17 reminds us, "Faith by itself, if it does not have works, is dead."

---

*A powerful example comes from Deborah in South Africa. Widowed with three children, her only income came from making handmade soaps. After hearing a sermon on 2 Kings 4, she created a plan, organized her workspace, and leaned on her church community. One year later, not only had she paid off her debts, but she also employed two other single mothers. She says, *"Pouring oil was only a miracle after I obeyed and started pouring."*

Planning, preventing, and producing are not just financial steps, they're faith steps. God worked a miracle through the widow as she followed the process. You don't need a big miracle to start, you need a plan, a closed door, and the courage to pour.

Planning won't feel exciting. Prevention will feel restrictive. Production will feel tiring. But these are the very disciplines God uses to rebuild lives. What feels slow in the moment becomes stability over time.

Let God work in your finances, but be ready to do your part.

For group discussion questions and personal reflection related to this chapter, please see the Small Group & Personal Study Guide in the Appendix.

Chapter 5: Sticking to the Plan

"So she went from him and shut the door behind her and her sons, who brought the vessels to her; and she poured it out. Now it came to pass, when the vessels were full, that she said to her son, 'Bring me another vessel.' And he said to her, 'There is not another vessel.' So the oil ceased."

2 Kings 4:5–6

The journey to becoming debt-free is not just a spiritual hope, it's a biblical strategy. We live in a world where debt is not only normalized but also nationalized. From personal credit cards to government deficits, debt is everywhere. But the Bible doesn't just warn against the dangers of debt; it provides a plan to escape it.

Most people don't fail financially because they don't start a plan, they fail because they don't stay with one. Discouragement, fatigue, impatience, and comparison slowly erode commitment.

In this study of "Breaking the Debt Ceiling," we've been examining how to limit our spending and operate within God-given financial boundaries. In this chapter, we turn our attention to the power of sticking to the plan.

The Weight of Debt

The Bible is a deeply practical book. While it certainly contains the miraculous, more often than not, it offers solutions that require our participation. Unfortunately, some believers disregard these practical steps because they seem "unspiritual." Many would rather wait for gold dust to fall from the ceiling or hope a wealthy relative wins the lottery than follow God's simple instructions.

Naaman, the commander of the Syrian army, exemplifies this resistance to the practical. When Elisha told him to wash in the Jordan River seven times to be healed of leprosy, Naaman was outraged. He expected spectacle, something grand, dramatic, supernatural (see 2 Kings 5:10–12). But his servants urged him to consider the simplicity of the prophet's instruction. Because he humbled himself and obeyed, he was healed (see 2 Kings 5:13–14).

The same principle applies to financial freedom. The answer often isn't a miracle but a change in behaviour. True transformation begins when we feel the full weight of our decisions. The widow in 2 Kings 4 had to actively participate in her own deliverance. She shut the door, gathered the vessels, and poured the oil. This took effort. It took time. It demanded obedience. And only when there were no more vessels did the oil cease (2 Kings 4:5–6).

This teaches us a powerful truth. God doesn't always swoop in to rescue us from financial messes. Sometimes He allows us to walk through the process, to feel the pain of past decisions, so we learn, grow, and change.

"Now no chastening seems to be joyful for the present, but painful; nevertheless, afterward it yields the peaceable fruit of righteousness to those who have been trained by it."
Hebrews 12:11

If God rescued us every time without allowing us to feel the consequences, we'd never learn. The process of getting out of debt involves pain, hard work, and active involvement. The widow's participation taught her, and teaches us, the value of change and the importance of staying engaged in the process. Next time, we may think twice before overspending or ignoring the budget.

Discipline in Scripture is never about restriction alone, it's about preparation. Athletes don't resent training; they embrace it because they understand the prize. Financial discipline is no different.

Sticking to the Plan

Freedom from debt is impossible without consistency. The widow had a plan, and she followed through. She didn't quit halfway or get distracted. She stuck with it until every vessel was filled.

"Now it came to pass, when the time had come for Him to be received up, that He steadfastly set His face to go to Jerusalem."

Luke 9:51

Like Jesus, we must set our face toward the goal. The objective is not just to reduce debt but to eliminate it. Too many people settle for partial victories, cutting their debt in half and calling it success. But the real victory is total freedom.

One couple discovered this firsthand. Living under the weight of student loans, credit card debt, and a car payment, they made the decision to cut back on unnecessary spending. One simple change? They gave up their daily coffee *shop visits, which added up to \$300 per month. Over a year, that amounted to \$3,600. In just under two years, they paid off their car loan early using the money they saved, simply by making coffee at home.*

It wasn't glamorous. There was no miracle windfall or surprise inheritance. But by sticking to a simple plan, they began walking in financial freedom. Their discipline was the key.

"Success is the sum of small efforts, repeated day in and day out."

—Robert Collier

Very few people abandon a financial plan in one decision. Most drift. A skipped budget meeting. A justified purchase. A small exception that becomes a new habit. Sticking to the plan requires vigilance, not perfection.

"Discipline is the bridge between goals and accomplishment."

—Jim Rohn

Finishing what we start requires discipline. The widow stuck to the plan. She didn't stop until the oil stopped. That's the image of faithfulness. It's the image of a person who is serious about financial change.

"For which of you, intending to build a tower, does not sit down first and count the cost… lest, after he has laid the foundation, and is not able to finish, all who see it begin to mock him?"

Luke 14:28–30

Must be committed to the goal, debt reduction, that means sticking to the plan.

"Most people fail, not because of lack of desire, but because of lack of commitment."

—Vince Lombardi

If you are halfway through your journey and tempted to stop, you are closer than you think. The widow didn't stop pouring when she was tired, she stopped when there were no vessels left. Fatigue is not failure. Stopping is.

God's Supernatural Power

The beauty of this story is not just in the widow's obedience, it's in God's response. He honoured her faith and her diligence. As she poured out what little she had, God poured in more than she could imagine.

"Now it came to pass, when the vessels were full…"

2 Kings 4:6

God's supernatural provision met her natural obedience. He didn't act until she did. And this is a critical point in biblical financial stewardship, God moves when we move. He joins our efforts, not our fantasies.

"When you do what you can, God will do what you cannot."

—Unknown

If we can be faithful in handling earthly resources, sticking to a plan, budgeting, living within our means, then God can entrust us with more. But it begins with us. He steps in when we step up.

"He who is faithful in what is least is faithful also in much... Therefore if you have not been faithful in the unrighteous mammon, who will commit to your trust the true riches?"

Luke 16:10–11

Getting out of debt is not a matter of chance, it's a matter of choice. God has given us both the wisdom of His Word and the strength of His Spirit to make sound financial decisions. The story of the widow reminds us that miracles often meet us in motion. She acted in obedience, poured out what little she had, and God met her there.

Your journey may feel slow, and the vessels may seem endless, but as you pour out faithfulness, budgeting, cutting back, staying disciplined, God pours in provision. Stick to the plan. Keep going. Every step of obedience is a step toward freedom.

"Do not grow weary while doing good, for in due season we shall reap if we do not lose heart."

Galatians 6:9

For group discussion questions and personal reflection related to this chapter, please see the Small Group & Personal Study Guide in the Appendix.

Chapter 6: Paying Your Debt

2 Kings 4:7

"Then she came and told the man of God. And he said, 'Go, sell the oil and pay your debt; and you and your sons live on the rest.'"

Every journey toward freedom reaches a moment of decision. After the oil was poured, the vessels filled, and the miracle complete, the widow still faced a choice. What she did next would determine whether the miracle ended in freedom or became another missed opportunity.

Debt is everywhere. Whether it's personal debt, national debt, or business debt, many people find themselves burdened under its weight. But the Bible offers a pathway to freedom, a clear plan for breaking the debt ceiling in our lives.

This chapter continues our study from 2 Kings 4:1–7, where a widow, desperate and in debt, encounters a miracle through the prophet Elisha. The miracle wasn't just about supernatural provision; it came with instructions. God's provision always comes with a purpose. This chapter, we look at what happens after the miracle, the instruction to pay your debt. This chapter is about that final, defining step, obedience.

Paying What We Owe

One of the clearest teachings in Scripture is that God expects us to pay what we owe. It's not enough to receive a breakthrough, we must follow through.

In 2 Kings 4:7, Elisha tells the widow, "Go, sell the oil and pay your debt; and you and your sons live on the rest."

"God gives every bird its food, but He does not throw it into its nest."

—J.G. Holland

This reminds us that God's provision requires action, like paying off debt.

John and Judy were in over $70,000 of debt, credit cards, personal loans, and car payments. After taking a financial peace course and getting serious about God's principles of stewardship, they sold one of their vehicles, stopped all unnecessary spending, and began aggressively paying down debt. When John received an unexpected bonus at work, it would have been easy to take a holiday or upgrade their car. Instead, they remembered the principle. "Pay what you owe." They used every dollar to pay down what they owed. Within two years, they were completely debt-free. They described the experience as "like being let out of prison." This story demonstrates the discipline and obedience required to honour God's instructions, even when other options seem more enjoyable.

The instruction was not vague or open to interpretation. It was direct, pay the debt. Yet, many people in real life, even after receiving a financial miracle or a significant blessing, do not follow this simple advice.

Some take the money meant to clear debt and spend it on a holiday or a new car. It's common to see people pay off one loan only to take out another, essentially swapping one chain for a different kind.

Others will pay only part of the debt and use the rest of the funds elsewhere. But God's Word challenges us to fully settle our debts, not to keep circling around financial bondage.

Paul echoes this in Romans 13:8 (NKJV), "Owe no one anything except to love one another, for he who loves another has fulfilled the law."

The widow's story teaches us that when God enables us to get free, we should use that opportunity wisely. Elisha's words in the New Century Version drive it home, "Go, sell the oil and pay what you owe. You and your sons can live on what is left." (2 Kings 4:7 NCV)

William Colgate, founder of Colgate-Palmolive, made a lifelong commitment to pay his debts and honour God with his money. As a young man, he found himself nearly bankrupt. But he began giving to God immediately, even when he had very little, and he worked hard to repay every obligation. Not only did he pay off his personal debts, but as his company grew, he began giving 10%, then 20%, and eventually over 50% of his income to God's work. He refused to live lavishly and never took on unnecessary debt again. Colgate's story is an example of someone who chose obedience and financial integrity over comfort or greed, and as a result, he left a legacy of blessing.

Paying what we owe is both a matter of obedience and spiritual maturity. It reflects good stewardship and a readiness to live in financial freedom.

God is not impressed by provision alone. He watches what we do with it. Obedience transforms provision into freedom.

Not every person who experiences God's help responds with obedience. Scripture records moments where blessing became breeding ground for pride rather than stewardship. God's provision tests us just as much as our lack.

King Hezekiah (2 Kings 20) is a classic example of God providing, and a man who did not steward that provision.

- God delivered him
- He mishandled blessing
- Pride followed

    - *"You can't pray away debt you willingly created and continue to support through poor stewardship."*

        - *—Unknown*

Living on the Rest

Freedom begins after the debt is paid. God didn't just help the widow pay off her debt, He gave her enough to live on. This is God's heart for us. He desires more than just freedom from bondage; He wants us to live, to thrive, and to enjoy the blessings He provides.

Living on the rest is not indulgence, it is alignment. It is living within God's provision without fear, pressure, or panic.

"He who is enslaved to debt is not free to follow God's call wherever it leads."

—Crown Financial Ministries

"Go sell the oil and make good on your debts. Live, both you and your sons, on what's left." 2 Kings 4:7 (The Message)

That word live is powerful. God doesn't want us constantly living pay check to pay check or burdened by bills. He wants us to be free.

Mary, a single mother in Texas, worked two jobs just to make ends meet. Buried in credit card debt, she prayed for a miracle. A church member helped her create a strict budget, and she sold unused furniture and electronics. Slowly, she began to pay off her debt.

When she finally cleared the last balance, she said, "I felt like I could breathe for the first time in years." What amazed her most was what came next, she received a promotion and a significant pay rise. For the first time, she had extra. She bought a reliable car (in cash!) and started a small savings fund for her son's college. Her story highlights how God not only helps us pay our debts, but blesses our obedience so that we can truly live on the rest.

But freedom doesn't come without responsibility. You cannot live freely while you're still enslaved by debt. Scripture is clear, "The rich rules over the poor, and the borrower is servant to the lender." Proverbs 22:7 (NKJV)

Debt controls more than your money, it controls your decisions, your opportunities, even your peace of mind. If you're a borrower, you don't fully control your life. Your choices are dictated by the terms of someone else's contract.

But once the debt is paid, you're free to live, not just exist, but to live.

"It is not God's will for His children to live under a spirit of bondage, but of liberty and blessing."

Adapted from Galatians 5:1

This idea of living in blessing is also found in Deuteronomy 28:1–13, where God outlines the blessings that come from obedience. These include fruitfulness, victory, abundance, and being "the head and not the tail." These blessings can't flow freely into lives trapped in disobedience or cycles of debt.

When you pay your debt, you position yourself for God's best. You align yourself with His plan for provision and peace.

"When the last bond is broken, the full blessing begins."

—Unknown

Authors and ministers Eric and Leslie Ludy began their marriage determined to remain debt-free. They lived simply, renting a small home, driving a used car, and carefully budgeting every expense. This allowed them to remain free from financial burdens and say "yes" when God called them into full-time ministry. Today, they've authored over a dozen books, run a discipleship program, and reach thousands of young people, all while living with financial integrity. Their story is a powerful example that freedom from debt opens the door to purpose, peace, and effectiveness in God's kingdom.

Final Reflection

God's financial miracle in your life is not just to rescue you, it's to reposition you. Once He provides the oil, the next step is obedience, pay the debt.

God never frees people merely so they can be comfortable. He frees them so they can be available. Once the widow's debt was paid, her sons were no longer at risk, they were free to build a future. Financial freedom restores options, generosity, responsiveness, and calling.

When we obey, we move from bondage to blessing. And when we follow God's principles, we can truly live on the rest, not just materially, but spiritually and emotionally free.

Debt is a form of slavery. But Jesus came to set us free. Use what He gives you not to prolong your captivity, but to pay what you owe and begin a new chapter of living in His freedom and abundance.

The oil has been poured. The vessels are full. The instruction is clear. Freedom is no longer a mystery, it's a decision. Pay what you owe. Close the chapter of bondage. Step into a future marked by integrity, peace, and purpose. This is not just financial wisdom. It is obedience.

For group discussion questions and personal reflection related to this chapter, please see the Small Group & Personal Study Guide in the Appendix.

Appendix: Small Group & Personal Study Guide

How to Use This Guide

This study guide is designed to help individuals and groups move from understanding to application. Each chapter includes:

- A **key theme**
- **Scripture focus**
- **Discussion questions**
- **Personal reflection**
- **Practical action step**

Take time with each section. Freedom is rarely instant, but it is always intentional.

Each study corresponds to a chapter in the book and includes:

- Key themes and Scriptures
- Discussion questions for small groups
- Personal reflection prompts
- Practical action steps

This guide may be used for:

- Home care or fellowship groups
- Men's and discipleship groups
- Financial foundations classes
- Individual personal study

Readers may work through the guide alongside the book or return to it after completing the main chapters.

"Stand fast therefore in the liberty by which Christ has made us free."
— Galatians 5:1

Study 1 — Debt Reality

Key Theme

Debt is not just a financial burden; it is a form of bondage that affects peace, purpose, and future.

Scripture Focus

- 2 Kings 4:1
- Proverbs 22:7
- Jeremiah 29:11

Discussion Questions

1. Why do you think debt has become so normal in today's culture?
2. How does the widow's situation reflect emotional as well as financial pressure?
3. What stood out to you about God's concern for people in debt?

Personal Reflection

- In what ways has debt affected your peace or decision-making?
- Have you ever felt trapped or powerless because of financial pressure?

Practical Action

Write down **all current debts**, without judgement or excuses. Honesty is the first step toward freedom.

Study 2 — What's in Your House?

Key Theme

God often begins miracles with what we already have, not what we lack.

Scripture Focus

- 2 Kings 4:2
- Exodus 4:2
- John 6:9

Discussion Questions

1. Why do people often say, "I have nothing," when facing financial stress?
2. What did God use in Moses' and the boy's hands?
3. How does fear distort our perception of what we possess?

Personal Reflection

- What skills, resources, or assets do you already have that you may have overlooked?
- What excuses have you been tempted to use?

Practical Action

Take inventory this week:

- Income
- Skills
- Assets
- Expenses

  Ask God, *"What can You use?"*

Study 3 — Moving Toward Freedom

Key Theme

Freedom begins when faith moves from intention to action.

Scripture Focus

- 2 Kings 4:3
- Joshua 3:13
- Proverbs 6:1–4

Discussion Questions

1. Why is movement often harder than intention?
2. What does it look like to prioritise debt elimination biblically?
3. How can relationships help or hinder financial freedom?

Personal Reflection

- Where have you delayed action out of fear or uncertainty?
- Who are the people influencing your financial decisions?

Practical Action

Identify **one clear step** you can take this week toward reducing debt.

Study 4 — Planning, Preventing, and Producing

Key Theme

God works through order, boundaries, and faithful effort.

Scripture Focus

- 2 Kings 4:4
- Proverbs 21:5
- Genesis 41:33–36

Discussion Questions

1. Why does planning often feel unspiritual to some believers?
2. What does "shutting the door" look like in modern life?
3. How does Joseph model biblical planning and prevention?

Personal Reflection

- What habits or behaviours threaten your financial progress?
- Are there boundaries you need to establish?

Practical Action

Create or review a **simple budget**. Identify one expense to reduce or eliminate.

Study 5 — Sticking to the Plan

Key Theme

Freedom is won through consistency, not enthusiasm.

Scripture Focus

- 2 Kings 4:5–6
- Hebrews 12:11
- Galatians 6:9

Discussion Questions

1. Why do people often quit halfway through financial change?
2. What does discipline look like biblically?
3. How does fatigue differ from failure?

Personal Reflection

- Where are you most tempted to drift or compromise?
- What has helped you stay consistent in other areas of life?

Practical Action

Recommit to your plan. Write down **why** freedom matters to you and review it daily.

Study 6 — Paying Your Debt

Key Theme

Obedience completes the miracle and opens the door to freedom.

Scripture Focus

- 2 Kings 4:7
- Romans 13:8
- Galatians 5:1

Discussion Questions

1. Why is paying debt a spiritual issue, not just a financial one?
2. What does it mean to "live on the rest"?
3. How does freedom create opportunity for generosity and purpose?

Personal Reflection

- How will your life change once debt is removed?
- What do you want freedom *for,* not just freedom *from*?

Practical Action

Set a **clear debt-elimination goal** and timeline. Pray over it and commit it to God.

Final Group Reflection

- What has God shown you through this study?
- What habits or mindsets must change permanently?
- How can this group support one another moving forward?

"Stand fast therefore in the liberty by which Christ has made us free."
— Galatians 5:1

Acknowledgements & Sources

Acknowledgements & Sources

The author gratefully acknowledges the following sources and contributors:

- Scripture quotations from the New King James Version (NKJV)
- Dave Ramsey – public financial teaching illustrations
- Crown Financial Ministries – principles of biblical stewardship
- William Colgate – historical example of debt-free stewardship
- Eric & Leslie Ludy – ministry testimony on financial integrity
- Various modern testimonies used for illustrative purposes

Other Books by the Author

- *Snapshots of Faith: The Book of Acts*
- *Snapshots of Faith: The Book of Joshua*
- *Snapshots of Faith: Great Challenges*
- *Snapshots of Faith: Winning Seasons*
- *Snapshots of Faith: Living Faithfully in a Fallen World*
- *Snapshots of Faith: Faith for the Future*
- *Financially Fit: Developing Habits That Lead to True Financial Wellness*
- *Sermon Notes from My Pastor: Volume 1*
- *Sermon Notes from My Pastor: Volume 2*
- *Sermon Notes from My Pastor: Volume 3*
- *Sermon Notes from My Pastor: Volume 4*
- *Sermon Notes from My Pastor: Volume 5*

Ministry & Contact

David welcomes correspondence, ministry connections, and feedback from readers.

Email:
phkalgoorlie@gmail.com

If this book has encouraged or helped you, please consider leaving a review. Your feedback helps others discover these biblical truths.

Made in United States
North Haven, CT
04 November 2026

21771553R00042